FIGHT FO
- The Batt

The "Battle of Britain, 1940" i
the intense air battles that we
Southern England, over the pe..... ... July to 31 October 1940.
It was waged by the Air Force, or "Luftwaffe", of Hitler's Nazi Germany who sought to destroy the Royal Air Force as an effective fighting force so that a seaborne invasion could be launched. It was also a battle without historical precedent as it was fought entirely in the air.

The Battle of Britain was one of the most crucial battles the UK has fought to date. If Britain had lost, a seaborne invasion would, probably, have been launched with overwhelming forces. The UK's means of waging war would have been destroyed by relentless bombing, and resistance overcome. Try to imagine life under Nazi occupation with the SS, Gestapo and concentration camps.

The Battle also had a profound effect on the outcome of the war, after the German armies invaded Russia in 1941. One of the most senior German Generals, Field Marshal Von Runstedt, was asked by the Russians, after the war, what was the most crucial battle they had fought. The Russians expected him to say Kursk, instead he said the Battle of Britain. They failed to defeat the UK in 1940 and had to fight on two fronts and so were unable to defeat Russia in 1941/42.

The aim of this booklet is to cover the high lights of the Battle and explain the decisive factors. It is based on talks given by the author to both lay and technically minded audiences.

1. PRELUDE TO THE BATTLE OF BRITAIN

The events which led up to the Battle of Britain in the summer of 1940 are briefly summarised below.
Great Britain and France declared war on Nazi Germany on 3 September 1939, following the German invasion of Poland in a highly effective "Blitzkreig" offensive. A large part of Poland was overrun, despite fierce resistance by the Polish army, when the Soviet Union, under Stalin's orders, invaded Poland from the East. This sealed Poland's fate and the country was conquered in five weeks and partitioned between Germany and Russia.

As in the First World War, the UK established a military force in France known as the "British Expeditionary Force", abbreviated usually to the "BEF". The BEF was deployed along the border between France and Belgium to cover the "Western Front" not defended by the "Maginot Line" of massive forts.

After the conquest of Poland, there was little or no military activity along the frontier between France and Germany, or "Western Front". The period from October 1939 to early March 1940, in fact, became known as the "Phoney War" in the popular press because of the inactivity. The German forces, however, were recovering and making good their losses in the Polish campaign and preparing for the massive Blitz they planned to launch in early May 1940 on the Western Front. The winter months of 1939/ 40 were exceptionally cold, and the snow and freezing conditions precluded any serious military operations.

This was all to change in early March when Hitler launched the German invasion of Norway and Denmark. Denmark was occupied without resistance. The small Norwegian army fought back, but was forced to retreat northwards leaving southern Norway in German hands. British forces were sent to Norway to assist the Norwegians but were inadequately equipped and had very little air cover. The Norwegian intervention was disastrous and the British forces had to be evacuated in early June 1940.

The war was going badly and the British Prime Minister, Neville Chamberlain, resigned. He was succeeded by Winston Churchill who became Prime Minister on 11 May 1940; an event which was to change the course of the war. The photograph, (Fig. 1), shows Winston Churchill in 1940 in a characteristic defiant pose with his "Tommy" gun. (Thompson sub-machine gun)

On 10 May 1940, Hitler launched a massive Blitzkreig on the Western Front with large, well equipped armies which invaded Holland, Belgium and France. The Blitzkrieg started with dawn raids on the French and British airfields and air bases in France and in Holland and Belgium. Large numbers of aircraft were destroyed on the ground before they could get airborne. The allied air forces had no radar warning systems and were taken by surprise. Belgium was overrun and occupied in three days and Holland in five days. Several hundred German tanks ("panzers") advanced through the Ardennes Forest in Belgium to take the French forces by surprise. The Forest had been assumed to be impassable for tanks!.

The Luftwaffe cooperated very closely with the army and air superiority enabled their Junkers Ju 87 "Stuka" dive bombers, to

(Photograph by courtesy of the Imperial War Museum, London   H2646A)

Fig.1 Winston Churchill, 1940

be called in to bomb any strongpoints impeding the advances with devastating accuracy. (Photo of Junkers 87 is shown on Page 42, Fig 23). The German armies, with their very large armoured forces, and dive bomber support, broke through the French defences and advanced deeply into France to encircle the French armies.

The attack through Belgium forced the BEF to retreat towards Dunkirk to avoid being cut off, following the German breakthrough in the Ardennes. The RAF light bomber squadrons, supporting the BEF, tried to stem the German advance through Belgium. They attacked targets with great bravery; sustaining nearly 90% losses on occasion. The Fairey "Battle" single engine light bomber, which they were mainly equipped with, was totally unsuited to this task.

It was too slow, inadequately armed, lacked manoeuvrability and only carried a 1,000 pound bomb load. Over 100 of the RAF Advanced Striking Force of light bombers were lost in the first four days of the offensive and the force was virtually wiped out in the following days.

The RAF Hurricane squadrons based in France (around 140 aircraft and around 200 pilots) acquitted themselves well.

They destroyed nearly 100 Luftwaffe aircraft, but were too few in number. They were flying six or seven sorties a day and were often outnumbered ten to one; they lost over half their strength in the first four days of the fighting.

Air Chief Marshal Sir Hugh Dowding, the Commander in Chief of Fighter Command, was ordered to send two full squadrons drawn from Fighter Command squadrons, to reinforce the Hurricane squadrons in France, in response to urgent appeals from the military. These were duly sent and on 14 May, the French Premier, Paul Reynaud, appealed for ten more RAF fighter squadrons to be sent over to France to support the crumbling French front line.

Dowding requested to attend the Cabinet Meeting on 15 May, and presented a simple graph showing the attrition rate over the previous two weeks and warned that, *"if the present rate of attrition continued for another fortnight, there would not be a single Hurricane left in France or in this country"*.

In spite of this, Dowding was ordered to send eight half strength squadrons to France leaving Fighter Command with just 36 fighter squadrons to defend the UK. On 16 May, he responded even more strongly and notified the Chief of the Air Staff, that it had been agreed that Fighter Command required a minimum of 52 squadrons to defend the UK and that if his defence force was drained away in desperate attempts to remedy the situation in France, it would result in the *"final, complete and irredeemable defeat of this country"*.

Three days later Churchill ruled that no more fighter squadrons should be sent to France. Dowding's intervention was crucial to the outcome of the Battle of Britain, which was, like the Duke of Wellington's comment on the Battle of Waterloo, *"a damn close run thing"*.

The German advance forced the RAF Hurricane squadrons to successively abandon their airfields and bases as the German army moved forward to encircle the BEF at Dunkirk. By late May1940, the BEF was encircled by the German army at Dunkirk.

On the 23 May, Goering promised the Luftwaffe would crush the evacuation and force the BEF to surrender. All out assaults on the troops and ships were accordingly launched by the Luftwaffe. The Royal Navy started the evacuation of the BEF on 26 May.

Air cover for the evacuation was provided by the fighter squadrons in South East England of No.11 Group of Fighter Command. The Commander in Chief of No 11 Group was Air Vice Marshal Sir Keith Park, a commander of outstanding ability. Park controlled his fighter squadrons with great skill in deploying them to deal with the Luftwaffe assaults. There were fierce air battles in the skies above the Dunkirk beaches which raged over several days while the evacuation took place and the RAF fighter pilots were flying three or four sorties a day on occasions. The RAF fighters greatly reduced these assaults and shot down over 130 German aircraft.

The RAF lost, however, over 100 aircraft and 80 pilots including a number of experienced and outstanding fighter pilots.

Inevitably, some of the Luftwaffe attacks got through and ships were sunk and troops bombed and strafed on the beaches. The RAF just did not have enough fighters to provide the cover required. This led to bitter recrimination and criticism of the RAF from the troops who had been bombed and strafed.

The Royal Navy and the small ships, however, were able to evacuate over one third of a million men.

This was the situation confronting Churchill three weeks after taking over as Prime Minister. If he had not become Prime Minister, it is very likely that peace terms would have been sought and there would not have been a Battle of Britain. By early June, the French had been defeated and had started to negotiate surrender terms. There was a significant faction, led by Lord Halifax, in the War Cabinet who wished to seek peace terms.

Churchill, to his eternal credit, was able to defeat these moves and was able to inspire the nation and revitalise morale.

Some readers may recall his speeches; like the one he made on the 7 June 1940 where he announced the Battle of Britain was now about to begin, and finishing with the stirring words

- *"We shall fight on the beaches - we shall fight on the landing grounds - we shall fight in the fields and in the streets - we shall fight in the hills - we shall never surrender".*

They were truly inspiring. The successful evacuation of over a third of a million men from the Dunkirk beaches made a great difference to national morale, although the men had had to leave their equipment behind.

France surrendered on 22 June 1940; about two thirds of the country was occupied by the German forces and about one third of the country was left under the control of a "puppet" French government based in Vichy, led by Marshal Petain, which collaborated totally with the Nazis.

On 3 July, the Royal Navy, acting on Churchill's orders, sank or badly damaged most of the French Fleet in Oran Harbour, North Africa. This was to prevent it falling into German hands and being used to support an invasion.

This finally put paid to any talk of peace terms. Up till then, Hitler had been utterly convinced that Britain would accept peace terms. He now realised this was not going to happen and in early July ordered the invasion of England to be planned for executing in September. The invasion was code named "Operation Sea Lion". Field Marshal Goering, the Commander in Chief of the Luftwaffe, promised to destroy the RAF as an effective force by the end of August, so that the seaborne invasion could be launched in September. (The German Army would not attempt an invasion without air supremacy, because of the Royal Navy.).

 The Battle of Britain was about to begin.

 A key decision Churchill made, soon after becoming Prime Minister, was to put Lord Beaverbrook in charge of all aircraft production. This was to have a vital influence on the outcome of the Battle. Beaverbrook was able to more than double aircraft production over the next three months. He also set up a very efficient repair organisation to repair battle damaged aircraft. He made a massive contribution to the successful outcome of the Battle. Thanks to his efforts, the RAF was never really short of fighter aircraft.

The man who was the architect of the country's survival in the Battle of Britain was Air Chief Marshal Sir Hugh Dowding, the Commander in Chief of Fighter Command.

The photograph of Sir Hugh Dowding, Fig.2, was taken in 1940 when he was 58 years old. He was a tall, lean man with a penetrating gaze. You can see from the photograph that he was not the sort to put up with any nonsense. He was a strict disciplinarian, but was a kindly man in private life.

He was an excellent administrator, very far sighted in his grasp of air warfare and he was able to delegate. He was also possessed of high intelligence. Put simply, he was able to out general his opposite numbers in the Luftwaffe.

 One of Dowding's key contributions to Fighter Command's success was the integrated Command and Control System he set up before the war for the air defence of Great Britain. This was the first command and control system for air defence in the world with an integrated radar warning system. It enabled the most efficient and effective interception of large scale attacks over a wide area of the UK, by the limited number of RAF fighters available, before the enemy aircraft had reached the targets. It was excellent.

 Another key contribution, for which Dowding was responsible, was the development of fast monoplane fighters armed with eight

(Photograph by courtesy of the Imperial War Museum, London   D1417)

Fig. 2 Air Chief Marshal Sir Hugh Dowding

machine guns (Hurricane and Spitfire). He sponsored their development soon after being made responsible for the Air Defence of Great Britain in 1935. The RAF had had a bias for highly manoeuvrable single seat biplane fighters and RAF fighter squadrons, in fact, were equipped with Hawker Fury and Gloster Gladiator biplane fighters until as late as 1938, and a few Gladiators were still in service in 1940. The Hurricane and Spitfire entered squadron service just in time.

Yet another key contribution was the development of the Radar Warning System. He sponsored its development and ensured top priority, after a successful demonstration of its potential in an experiment, which he had requested. The UK would have lost the Battle of Britain, if it hadn't had an effective radar warning system.

He was also able to stop Churchill sending fighter squadrons to France in early June; a crucial decision as mentioned earlier.

Dowding also got on very well with Lord Beaverbrook. Although very different in character, each respected the other's abilities. Both were totally dedicated to serving the country above all else. Each had a son who was a fighter pilot in the Battle of Britain. (Both sons, fortunately, survived the war.)

2. THE UNITED KINGDOM AIR DEFENCE SYSTEM

The integrated Command and Control System of Fighter Command was vital to the RAF's success. This was because it enabled the most effective use to be made of the very limited numbers of fighter pilots and fighters available to defend the whole of the United Kingdom from mass assaults attacking targets over widely separated regions of the UK.

By early August 1940, the Luftwaffe could deploy three Air Fleets with a total of around 3,000 aircraft against the UK. These comprised around 1,200 medium range twin engine bombers, around 400 single engine "Stuka" dive bombers and around 1100 fighters; the rest being reconnaissance, transport and long range anti shipping aircraft. Two of the Air Fleets were based in France and one was based in Norway.

Fighter Command, at that time, had fifty four fighter squadrons comprising about 700 aircraft to defend the UK. A normal fighter squadron comprised 12 aircraft and 18 pilots. Not all the squadrons were fully up to strength and not all these aircraft were available at any one time.

There were twenty seven squadrons equipped with Hawker Hurricane single seat fighters and nineteen squadrons equipped with Vickers Supermarine Spitfire single seat fighters. The combined total of high performance fighters capable of taking on the Luftwaffe aircraft at the start of the Battle of Britain was thus around 550, barely sufficient. (The Hurricane and Spitfire are reviewed later in the booklet.)

There were also two squadrons equipped with the Boulton Paul Defiant single engine, two seat fighter and six squadrons equipped with fighter versions of the Bristol Blenheim twin engine bomber. The Blenheims were mainly operated as night fighters. Neither the Defiant, nor the Blenheim, made a significant contribution in the Battle of Britain as they lacked the speed and manoeuvrability required for a daytime fighter. The Defiant squadrons, in fact, sustained such heavy losses in the early phase of the Battle that they were progressively withdrawn and converted to a night fighter role. A Blenheim night fighter equipped with Airborne Interception Radar did, however, make the world's first radar interception at night and shot down a Heinkel He111 bomber in July 1940.

The integrated command and control system was organised as follows. The United Kingdom was split into four regions as shown in Figure 3; the South West, South East, Midlands and the North. Each region was assigned a Group to defend it.

Fig. 3 RAF Fighter Command Group Regions

The South West was covered by 10 Group under the command of Air Vice Marshal Sir Quintin Brand. Brand had two squadrons of Hurricanes and two squadrons of Spitfires to perform this task.

The South East was covered by 11 Group and was commanded by Air Vice Marshal Sir Keith Park.
11 Group had thirteen squadrons of Hurricanes, six squadrons of Spitfires and three squadrons of Blenheims.

The Midlands was covered by 12 Group, commanded by Air Vice Marshal Sir Trafford Leigh Mallory. They had six squadrons of Hurricanes, five squadrons of Spitfires, one squadron of Defiant two seat fighters and one Blenheim squadron.

The North was covered by 13 Group, commanded by Air Vice Marshal Sir Richard Saul. He had six squadrons of Hurricanes, six squadrons of Spitfires, one squadron of Defiants and one squadron of Blenheims to defend the whole of the North of the UK. The jam had to be spread thinly, as the saying goes.
Each Group had its own Head Quarters which controlled the sector airfields in its region; the whole region being split into sectors like slices of a cake. All four Groups were in turn controlled from Fighter Command Headquarters at Bentley Priory, Stanmore, Middlesex. The communication links were made by telephone and tele-printer. The heart of the system was the Command and Control Centre at Fighter Command Headquarters.

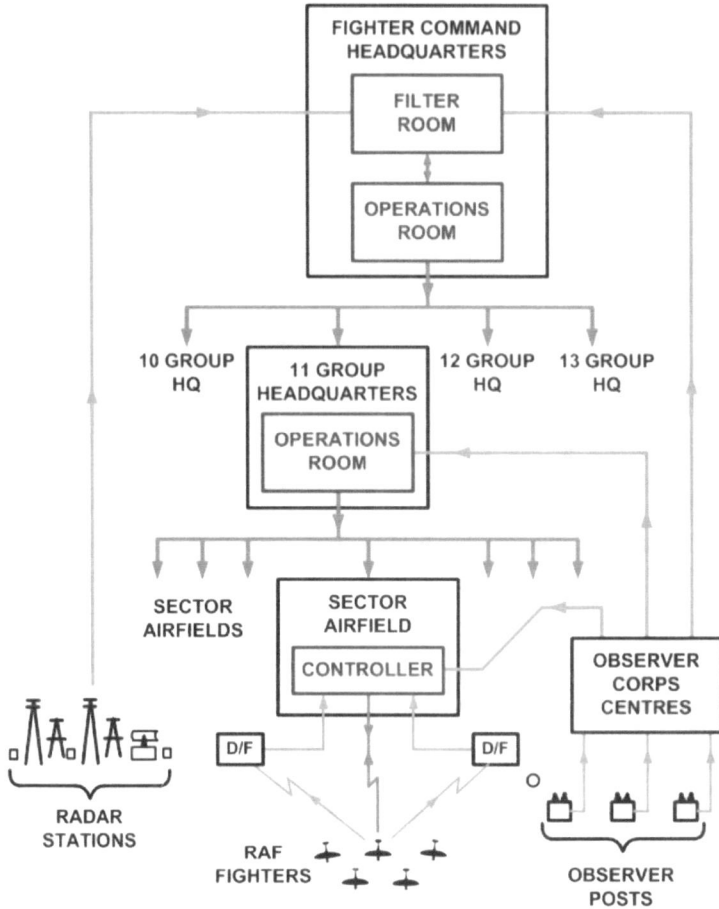

Fig. 4 Command & Control System of RAF Fighter Command

Figure 4 shows the integrated Command and Control System of RAF Fighter Command. The information from the Radar Stations and the Observer Corps Centres was first plotted and filtered in the Filter Room before being passed to the Operations Room next door. Both rooms were underground for protection. Commands and filtered information on the attacking forces were then sent over the telephone links to all the Group Headquarters.

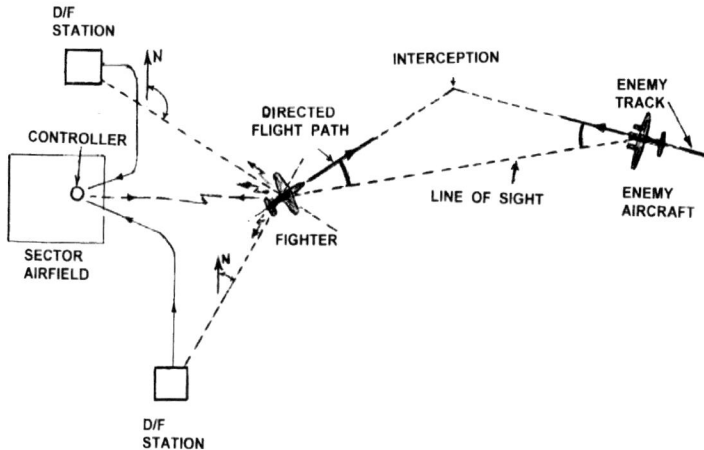

Fig. 5   Ground Control Interception – "Vectoring"

These had similar versions of the Operations Room at Fighter Command Headquarters at Bentley Priory.
The information was also sent to the Army Anti -Aircraft Gun Batteries which were an integral part of the air defence system.
(This has been left off Figure 4 for clarity).

The information on the numbers of enemy bombers and fighters, their position and the direction they were heading was then plotted on the Group Headquarters plotting table and updated continuously and sent to the Sector Airfields. (Note painting of 11 Group Operations Room on the back cover)). Group Headquarters would then order the Sector Airfields to intercept the enemy aircraft. The Sector Airfield Controller ordered the squadrons to take off and gave the guidance instructions to the fighters over the radio telephone so as to make an interception.

The Ground Controlled Interception process became known as "vectoring" and is illustrated in Fig.5. The position and track of the enemy aircraft were plotted and updated from the radar information and the sightings made by the Observer Corps Posts. The position of the intercepting fighters was determined as follows. The fighter's radio transmitter (R/T) was automatically switched on for 14 seconds every minute to transmit an individually coded radio frequency (RF) signal; when the pilot was not using the R/T. The system was known as "Pip Squeak". These RF transmissions enabled the position of the intercepting fighters to be determined from the bearings obtained by a chain of High Frequency Direction Finder (HF/DF) stations on the ground, usually referred to as "Huff Duff" stations. These were linked by telephone directly to the Sector Airfield Controller and the radio D/F bearings plotted on the Plotting Table. The intersection of these bearing lines giving the fighter's position. (A process referred to as "triangulation").

Referring to Fig. 5, the Line of Sight from the fighter to the enemy aircraft is known as the "Target Sight Line". The Controller directed his fighters to fly along a flight path, or vector, which made an angle with the Target Sight Line equal to the angle between the Target Track and the Target Sight Line, like an isosceles triangle.
This vectoring technique had been discovered empirically on a pre- war exercise; it was easy to use and avoided the need for a relatively complex electro-mechanical analogue computer.

There were serious shortcomings in the operation of the Command and Control System in its early days. Shortly after the outbreak of war in September 1939, two squadrons of fighters had been vectored on to each other following a reported sighting of unidentified aircraft over the Thames Estuary. Two Hurricanes were shot down by Spitfires in the melee and confusion and, sadly, the pilot of one was killed. Keith Park, the C in C of No. 11 Group, held an enquiry into this fiasco, which became known unofficially as the "Battle of Barking Creek". As a result those involved were severely disciplined and stringent disciplines and operating procedures instituted. By the time the Battle started, the system was running efficiently and effectively.

It is interesting to look at the RAF's integrated Command and Control System in 1940 from a present day perspective. The system configuration is basically similar in essence to that of a modern "Network Centric" system. In a modern system, all the "assets" as they are termed, for example, ground radars, airborne early warning radars are all linked through digital data networks, including satellite communication links. This information is processed by batteries of interlinked digital computers and displayed on large electronic display panels.

In 1940, communication links were by telephone. The computers were that extremely powerful and intelligent computer – the human brain! The situation was displayed on large plotting tables which were continuously updated manually. All in all, the system was relatively simple, very robust and flexible. The speed of response was, of course, much slower and would be totally inadequate with present day threats. There is also much more information to deal with and process and computers are absolutely essential.

2. 1 Radar or "RDF"

Radar was the key element in the interception chain and was developed just in time before the war. It was called "RDF", Radio Direction Finding, as a cover to hide its real purpose. (The name "radar", which is an acronym of the first letters of "**Ra**dio **D**irection **a**nd **R**ange", did not come into use until later in the war.) Radar was of immense value and the RAF would have lost the Battle without it. It was able to detect aircraft up to 100 miles away. The RAF were able to detect the German aircraft as they were being assembled into large formations over their bases and then track them all the way till they crossed the coast.

The early radars, however, had fixed transmitting and receiving antennae which pointed out to sea and could not function once the coastline had been crossed. They were crude compared with later radars and just good enough.

A chain of twenty one radar stations, known under the code name "Chain Home" stations (CH), was installed round the coast of Great Britain. The CH radar operated at the relatively low transmission frequency (by radar standards) of around 30 MHz. This corresponds to a wavelength of around 10 metres and resulted in relatively large antennae mounted on tall masts. (Antenna dimensions are directly proportional to the wavelength.) Figures 6 is photograph showing the Chain Home radar station installed at Dover. The very tall transmitter masts can be seen. These masts were 360 ft. high and were a steel girder structure. The receiver masts were 240 ft. high and were located some distance away and were a wood built structure.

The transmitter and receiver electronic equipment and operators were housed in separate wooden huts near the transmitter and receiver masts. Figure 7 is a photograph showing the airmen and WAAF operators at work in the Receiver Hut of a CH radar station.

The CH stations gave good coverage up to 25,000 ft. but were unable to detect low flying aircraft. To overcome this problem, a new radar known as "Chain Home Low" (CHL) had been developed which operated at 200 MHz.
This corresponds to a wavelength of 1.5 metres, enabling a smaller trainable transmitter antenna to be used. The CHL transmitter antenna was mounted on top of a 130 foot high mast. The receiver antenna was mounted on the ground. The trainable antenna enabled much more accurate target bearing information to be obtained. The Chain Home Low stations had a range of over 100 miles and were able to detect aircraft down to 500 ft. altitude.

Fig. 6 "Chain Home" (CH) Radar Station

Fig. 7 Airmen & WAAF Operators in CH Receiver Hut

The first CHL station was not installed until November 1939, but by July 1940 there were twenty nine CHL stations in operation. Just in time! There were also mobile radars based on the CHL radar.

The radar information from the different radars was combined to make use of the best characteristics of the individual radars. For example, a technique known as "Range Cutting" was used to combine the range information from two adjacent CH radar stations to provide an accurate bearing and position. This process was carried out on the Plotting Table by drawing an arc of a circle from adjacent radar stations, with a radius equal to the respective target ranges. The intersection of the two arcs gives the target's bearing and position. The CH radars gave very accurate range measurement but less accurate bearing information; Range Cutting thus overcame this deficiency.

All RAF aircraft carried equipment known as the "IFF", "Identification Friend or Foe" set. This sent back a coded identification signal when illuminated by the radar and enabled the radar operators to distinguish hostile aircraft from RAF aircraft.

. Watson Watt, later Sir Robert Watson Watt, who was responsible for British radar development, had two phrases he used to quote:

"The best is the enemy of the good", and *"Second best tomorrow"*. How right he was for the Battle of Britain in 1940.

2. 2 The Observer Corps

Once the enemy aircraft crossed the coastline, the Observer Corps, later to become the Royal Observer Corps, took over the task of detecting and tracking the enemy aircraft visually.

Dowding referred to them as his "Mark 1 Eyeball System". There were over 1,000 Observer Corps Posts covering the whole of the UK. They were manned by over 30,000 part time volunteers. The typical Observer Post, Fig. 8, was manned by two Observers equipped with a simple theodolite for measuring the bearing and elevation angles of the aircraft. (Measuring the angle of elevation of the aircraft enabled the aircraft height to be estimated as the aircraft appeared over known distances and land marks.)

The information from the Observer Corps Posts was phoned through to the Observer Corps Centre for the region for collation and filtering. Figure 9 shows a typical Observer Corps Centre. The collated and filtered sightings were then phoned through to Fighter Command Headquarters at Bentley Priory and the Group Headquarters and Sector Airfields. (Refer to Fig. 4.)

The Observer Corps had a vital role in the Battle of Britain and carried out their task in an exemplary way.

(Photograph by courtesy of the Imperial War Museum, London   CH 8215)

Fig. 8   Typical Observer Corps Post

(Photograph by courtesy of the Imperial War Museum, London   CH 11756)

Fig. 9   Typical Observer Corps Centre

3 THE BATTLE OF BRITAIN, JULY to OCTOBER 1940

The man who controlled the air defence of South East England, where most of the Battle was fought, was Air Vice Marshal Sir Keith Park, the Commander in Chief of No.11 Group.

(Photograph by courtesy of the Imperial War Museum, London   CM 3513)

Fig. 10 Air Vice Marshal Sir Keith Park

Park was 48 years old in 1940. He was a New Zealander and had been a fighter pilot ace in WW1 and had been awarded the DFC and MC; in a word, he was brilliant.

Figure 10 is a photograph of Sir Keith Park beside his own personal aircraft which he used to visit his squadrons in the field. He was very popular with his squadrons.

Park was a superb tactician and didn't put a foot wrong. He was always able to spot the real threats and make the best use of his squadrons to respond to them. His part in providing effective air cover for the successful evacuation of one third of a million men from the Dunkirk beaches was mentioned earlier.

At the start of the Battle, the RAF had around 550 serviceable single seat fighters, as mentioned earlier. They had lost over 500 fighters, mainly in the fighting in France and over the Dunkirk beaches, and a small number in the Norwegian campaign.

435 fighter pilots had been lost; either killed or missing, or captured. Fighter Command's strength was nearly 50% lower than it had been two months earlier.

At any one time, a further 100 or so aircraft could be undergoing servicing, or undergoing repair, or having essential modifications incorporated, or having defects / malfunctions rectified which had been reported by the pilots.

Over two thirds of the fighter force was equipped with Hurricanes and just under one third with Spitfires, as mentioned earlier.

There was also a force of around 60 serviceable Blenheim fighters which were mainly used in a night fighter role and around 25 serviceable Defiant single engine two seat fighters armed with a four gun power operated turret. Fighter Command had a total of around 1,200 fighter pilots at the start of the Battle..

The German Luftwaffe was not at full strength in early July after recovering from the campaign in France and was busy deploying its squadrons to new bases near the Channel coast and would not be ready to launch an all-out assault on the RAF until early August.

Goering, however, was keen to make a start in early July on a smaller scale to draw the RAF into combat and start a process of attrition. Goering's subsequent decisions were to have a major influence on the outcome of the Battle of Britain.

It is appropriate to briefly discuss the Luftwaffe leader at this point of the narrative. Figure 11 is a photograph of Field Marshal Herman Goering in 1940, accompanied by the outstanding ace fighter pilot and tactician, Werner Molders.

Goering not only held the rank of Field Marshal, but he also held the even higher rank of "Reichmarschall", and was Hitler's designated successor. Goering had been an ace fighter pilot in the First World War and had been awarded the coveted decoration "Pour le Merite" for bravery. He had succeeded Von Ricthofen, (the" Red Baron"), in command of the celebrated "Flying Circus", when Von Richthofen was killed.

He was regarded as a "war hero" and was a founder member of the Nazi Party. Goering's ability and ruthlessness enabled him to rise rapidly in the Nazi Party and hold an extremely powerful position when the Nazi Party came to power in 1933. He formed the Gestapo and set up the first concentration camps and remained a dedicated Nazi to the end of his life.

Goering was a complex man; he embraced a very luxurious life style .but was a lot tougher than he appeared. He was an intelligent man, but a combination of arrogance and ignorance of modern air warfare and technology were to result in him making a number of strategic and tactical errors in the subsequent Battle which had a major influence on the outcome.

The Battle of Britain progressed through four distinct phases which are described in the following sub sections

(Photograph by courtesy of the Imperial War Museum, London .HU 8481)

Fig.11 Field Marshal Herman Goering
& Oberst Lieutenant Werner Molders

3.1 The First Phase of the Battle
10 July to 7 August 1940 - *"The Channel War"*

The start of the Battle of Britain began in earnest on the 10th July 1940 with bombing attacks, including dive bombing, on shipping and convoys in the Channel and the Channel ports; including the naval base at Portsmouth. Coastal shipping formed a vital part of the UK's transport system. Goering's aim was to force the RAF into combat to defend the shipping and ports and whittle down their forces before the main assault. These attacks were carried out for nearly a month, but were inconclusive.

The Luftwaffe lost 274 aircraft in these attacks. The RAF losses totalled 124 aircraft. Eighty experienced squadron and flight commanders, however, had been lost.

3. 2 The Second Phase of The Battle
12 August to 7 September 1940
"All-out assault on RAF Fighter Command"

Following this first phase, Goering switched his forces to a massive assault on RAF Fighter Command to attain air supremacy by bombing the fighter airfields and aircraft factories.

19

This would force the RAF into combat, and he aimed to destroy Fighter Command as an effective fighting force by a process of attrition. He promised Hitler air supremacy by the end of August. He called his plan "Eagle Attack".

The first major assault of this new phase began on the on 12 August with the prime aim of blinding the radar system. Radar stations were attacked with considerable success creating large holes in the radar screen for further attacks to get through. The CH radar station at Ventnor on the Isle of Wight was hit by dive bombing Junkers 88's and badly damaged. A mobile radar station was used to fill the gap while the CH station was repaired.

Goering and the Luftwaffe chiefs then made a major blunder. They did not fully understand the importance of the radar stations and concluded that they were not particularly vulnerable and not worth major assaults

The CH radar stations were difficult to dive bomb without crashing into the masts, and the fact that the radar stations were very quickly back in operation led to these conclusions. In fact, the huts which housed the radar operators and transmitter and receiver electronics were highly vulnerable. The Luftwaffe assumed the RAF would have the operators and equipment underground.

There were no more concentrated and intensive assaults on the chain of radar stations. Sporadic attacks, however, were made on individual radar stations and they also started jamming the radar transmissions in late August. Generally, a skilled radar operator could still pick out the moving enemy aircraft "blips" on the cathode ray tube display from all the jamming "grass" and noise.

Goering designated the day for the launch of the massive assault on Fighter Command as "Eagle Day". This was originally planned for the13th August, but this day turned out to be a shambles for the Luftwaffe. A large scale attack planned for the morning was cancelled at the last minute because of the weather. The first wave of bombers, however, had taken off early and never received the recall signal because their radios had the wrong frequency crystal installed! They set off without fighter escort and were decimated by the RAF.

They launched major attacks on unimportant airfields in the afternoon. Detling and Middle Wallop airfields were blitzed and a considerable number of aircraft were destroyed and 70 RAF ground staff killed. The main sector airfields, however, were untouched. The Luftwaffe lost 39 aircraft; the RAF lost 14.

The 15th August now became "Eagle Day" – it was subsequently known in the Luftwaffe as "Black Thursday" because of the losses

Fig. 12 Flight Lieutenant James Nicolson VC

they received. Goering planned three massive assaults by three Air-Fleets, each comprising large bomber formations with a large fighter escort. Two of the Air-Fleets were based in France and were to attack airfields and aircraft factories in the South East and the South West of England respectively. The third Air-fleet was based in Norway and was to attack airfields and aircraft factories in the North of England. It all went badly wrong for the Luftwaffe; again effort was wasted attacking secondary airfields.

The attack from Norway was decimated. In fact, the Norway based Air Fleet was so badly mauled that it took no further part in daylight operations during the Battle.

Luftwaffe losses were 77 aircraft against 32 for the RAF.

The next day, 16th August, saw further intensive attacks on the airfields. Considerable damage was done and a number of aircraft were destroyed on the ground.

The bravery of the RAF fighter pilots was demonstrated that day by Flight Lieutenant James Nicolson, Fig. 12, who was subsequently awarded the Victoria Cross. He was wounded and his Hurricane on fire from an attack by Messerschmitt 109's and had started to climb out of the cockpit, when a Messerschmitt 110 appeared in his flight path. He climbed back into the blazing cockpit to shoot down the Me110 before baling out. He was badly burned but survived, but very sadly was killed in a flying accident later in the war.

Fig. 13 Map showing location of 11 Group Sector Airfields

(Fighter Command HQ and Group HQ's are denoted by Triangles)

Forty four Luftwaffe aircraft were shot down and 21 aircraft damaged. The RAF lost 24 aircraft including the aircraft destroyed on the ground.

The 17 August was a quiet day.

The 18 August 1940 has been called the "hardest day" of the Battle of Britain by the RAF. Large numbers of enemy aircraft made intensive low and medium level attacks on airfields in the South East of England, (see Fig. 13), throughout the day. Biggin Hill and West Malling airfields in Kent and Kenley and Croydon airfields in Surrey were attacked.

Kenley airfield was badly hit, aircraft on the ground were destroyed and it was temporarily out of action.

The Coastal Command base at Thorney Island and the Fleet Air Arm station at Ford in Sussex were also attacked.

The Luftwaffe lost 67 aircraft, including 17 Junkers Ju 87 "Stuka" dive bombers, while 35 more aircraft were damaged.

The Stuka dive bomber losses were, in fact, so severe that they took no further part in the Battle of Britain.

The RAF lost 36 aircraft, three of these aircraft were destroyed on the ground and 22 aircraft were damaged but repairable. Ten pilots were killed and 22 pilots were wounded, some seriously.

Despite this success, it was inevitably becoming a war of attrition which Fighter Command would lose. They just did not have enough experienced fighter pilots. Although losses of aircraft had been largely made up by new and repaired fighters, this increasing loss rate could not be withstood for long.

Both sides reviewed their tactics after this.

Dowding and Park issued instructions to concentrate on attacking the bombers and to avoid fighter to fighter combat as much as possible in order to conserve their forces.

Goering made a major blunder after the Luftwaffe bomber crews complained bitterly about their losses on the 15 August. He issued instructions that in future the fighters were to fly alongside the bomber formations and stay close to them. This reduced their effectiveness as it took away a major tactical advantage of surprise attacks from above. Up till then, they had used what they called "Free Hunt" tactics, flying free ranging sorties above the bombers. They waited for the chance to dive down out of the sun onto the RAF fighters when they were engaged in attacking the Luftwaffe bombers. An attack from above, particularly if the target has not seen the attacker until the last minute, is highly effective.

A height advantage is what all fighter pilots seek.

Apart from the loss of the tactical advantage, Goering's directive further reduced the effectiveness of the fighter escort. This was because the Luftwaffe's principal fighter, the Messerschmitt Me.109E, had a very limited endurance. Keeping position with a much slower moving bomber formation, and having to weave backwards and forwards to do so, used up a lot of fuel. The result was there was only enough fuel for 12 minutes of combat before the Me.109's had to turn back or risk running out of fuel and "ditching" in the Channel. (It should be appreciated that flying flat out uses up a lot of fuel.). Very fortunately, the Germans did not have a version of the Me.109 E with jettison-able external fuel tanks, or drop tanks" as they are usually called, until late August 1940, and not in sufficient numbers to count.

The major problem facing Fighter Command was the shortage of experienced fighter pilots. All too often, young pilots were being sent to the operational squadrons with very few flying hours experience in the Spitfire or Hurricane. The result was that many were shot down in their first few combats.

On occasion, their first combat was also their last. The Luftwaffe, by contrast, had a large number of experienced fighter pilots with combat experience.

The last two weeks of August and the first week in September saw an intensification of the attacks on the vital sector airfields.

The sheer intensity of the attacks was taking its toll of the RAF fighter pilots who were becoming very tired and physically exhausted from the strain of flying three or four combat sorties a day without let up. It should be appreciated that there is a great physical effort required to manoeuvre an aircraft when accelerations of four to five "g" are experienced during turns, or pulling out of a dive. The pilot is being forced down into his seat with a force of four to five times his own weight during such manoeuvres; the blood is being drained from his brain and he is on the edge of "blacking - out" and losing consciousness.

The aerodynamic forces acting on the control surfaces increase rapidly as the airspeed increases, so that the pilot needs to exert large forces on the stick and rudder bar to control the aircraft.

Dowding was trying to rotate the squadrons and take them out of the main battle area and rest them, when possible, but there just weren't enough pilots. By early September, Fighter Command was reeling; four of the seven key sector airfields in the South-East were badly damaged and were only partly operational.

Hitler, meanwhile, had set 24 September for "Operation Sea Lion", the invasion of England, provided air supremacy had been obtained and the RAF was no longer an effective force.

The "Big Wing" controversy advocated by AVM Trafford Leigh-Mallory, who was Commander in Chief of 12 Group, and his ace pilot, Wing Commander Douglas Bader, arose during late August. They believed that a large number of fighters in "Wings" of 50 to 100 aircraft should be assembled before attacking the enemy; - a "Wing" comprises several squadrons.

This sounds a good idea, but in practice there was insufficient time to assemble several squadrons into a Wing. It took over 16 minutes to climb to 18,000 ft. and interceptions had to be made by around 20 to 30 aircraft, or not at all. An acrimonious dispute arose between Park and Leigh- Mallory; Park complaining bitterly that when he sought help from the adjacent 12 Group to defend his airfields, they always arrived too late.

Having got so near to gaining air supremacy, Hitler and the Luftwaffe Command blew it. They switched from attacking the key sector airfields in the South-East to an all-out Blitz on London on 7 September.

3. 3 The Third Phase of the Battle
7 September to 30 September 1940 - *"The Blitz on London"*

Goering thought that RAF Fighter Command was virtually finished as an effective fighting force at the end of August. Massive bombing raids day and night on London would bring the nation to its knees and there would be no need for an invasion.

The Luftwaffe, however, had grossly under-estimated the strength of RAF Fighter Command The German fighter pilots had claimed more than twice the number of RAF fighters than had actually been shot down. German Intelligence had also completely under-estimated the numbers of new fighters being produced by Britain. The effectiveness of the British repair organisation in repairing battle damaged aircraft and restoring them to operational condition had also been ignored.

Hitler was also incensed, to put it mildly, by the bombing of Berlin which had started on the 26 August 1940, on Churchill's orders. This was in reprisal following the accidental release of some bombs on London by a Luftwaffe bomber. Over 80 RAF aircraft from Bomber Command attacked Berlin but did little damage. Subsequent raids in the next few days, however, did some damage. Hitler endorsed the massive Blitz on London and gave the go ahead to Goering.

The day and night Blitz on London started on 7 September 1940 and the attacks on the airfields ceased. London endured a savage bombing, particularly on the East End and Docks area. Huge fires raged where warehouses and fuel storage tanks had been hit. Over 400 civilians were killed and over 1,600 civilians severely injured on that night.

The switch in tactics on 7 September, from attacking the key sector airfields to an all-out day and night Blitz of London was to prove a decisive factor in the outcome of the Battle of Britain.

More raids followed in the next few days but were less intense because of bad weather.

Goering planned to launch a massive all-out blitz on London on 15 September to deliver the knock-out blow which would result in Britain's submission.

The one week break from the airfield attacks from 7 September to 15 September, however, proved to be a godsend for RAF Fighter Command.

"A week is a long time in a war", to adapt the former British Prime Minister, Harold Wilson's phrase about politics.

Park was able to repair the sector airfields, restore all the telephone lines and get back to full operational effectiveness. Fighter Command had had a break and Dowding was able to make some fresh pilots available.

September 15 was the decisive day of the Battle of Britain. Very large assaults of over 350 German bombers escorted by more than 600 fighters were launched in the morning and afternoon on London together with a diversionary raid on Portsmouth.

Dowding, for once, was able to commit all of the available Fighter Command squadrons to repel these assaults.

Leigh-Mallory's "Big Wing", of nearly 100 fighters from 12 Group, was able to arrive in time, on this occasion, thanks to the wind speed and direction which assisted their progress and slowed down the Luftwaffe aircraft. They were able to make a major contribution in both the morning and afternoon attacks. The bomber formations were broken up and the Luftwaffe pilots were staggered by the strength of the RAF response.

They had been told that the RAF was down to their last 50 fighters!

At the end of the day, the RAF had shot down 56 German aircraft for the loss of 29 aircraft and 12 pilots killed. At the time, it was believed that as many as 185 German aircraft had been shot down. The true figures only became clear when the Luftwaffe records became available after the war. It would be easy with the large melees and numbers of combats taking place at the same time for more than one fighter to score hits on the same aircraft. The pilot would think he had made the "kill", when it was seen to be going down. Several pilots could thus claim the same aircraft.

The "Big Wing" paid off on this occasion, as it convinced the German High Command of the strength and effectiveness of the RAF. They realised that they would not be able to attain air superiority in time to launch an invasion before the weather window closed with the approach of winter.

On 17 September, Hitler ordered Operation Sea Lion to be stood down indefinitely. The daylight raids continued after the 15 September; some were large scale but of lower intensity.

3. 4 The Fourth Phase - 1 October to 31 October 1940
"The End of the Battle"

By early October 1940, the Luftwaffe raids had started to tail off. Attacks were made with high flying fighter-bombers, including Me.109 fighter-bombers fitted with external "drop tanks" carrying additional fuel. They were difficult to intercept but did little damage.

By the end of October 1940, the Battle of Britain was over. The Battle had been won against all the odds; the Luftwaffe had failed to gain air supremacy. RAF Fighter Command was still intact and growing stronger than ever.

Hitler decided he would force the UK into submission by all-out nightly blitzes on the major cities in conjunction with a major U-boat offensive on the merchant ship convoys which the UK depended on for vital supplies. This would sever the country's essential supplies and result in starvation.

The Battle of the Atlantic had begun.

In the meantime, Hitler and his Generals got on with planning the invasion of Russia. The nightly blitz on London and other major cities continued until May 1941 and finally ceased with the invasion of Russia in June 1941. A major part of the Luftwaffe's forces were then committed to the Russian front.

The rest is history, as they say.

4 TACTICS AND LESSONS

It is appropriate at this point to discuss and explain some of the tactics and lessons learned during the Battle which had a major impact on the subsequent outcome.

4.1. Tactical formations.

The RAF fighter squadrons were greatly handicapped initially by their tactical use of tight formations in a series of choreographed manoeuvres to carry out an attack on the enemy bomber formations. These manoeuvres had been devised in the early 1930s and were totally unsuited to the situation in 1940. They took no account of the much higher speeds of the aircraft and the defence of the bombers by the large numbers of modern high performance single seat fighters escorting them
.Figure 14 shows Hurricanes in typical tight V formations. The tight formations caused the pilots to spend much of their time concentrating on maintaining position in the formation instead of looking round in all directions scanning the sky for enemy fighters. As a result, many were attacked from behind by Messerschmitt Me.109's they had not seen. The first they knew about it was being hit by bullets or cannon shells, or if they were lucky, shells or bullets shooting by. The RAF expression for experiencing this unexpected surprise attack is being "bounced".

Fig.14   Nine Hurricanes of 85 Squadron in "V" formation

Initially the RAF tried to counter this by delegating three aircraft in the formation to act as "weavers", weaving to and fro behind the formation to warn them of a rear attack. The German tactics were to "bounce" the weavers and then "bounce" the formation.

The Luftwaffe, however, had developed very loose formations based on four aircraft flying in two widely separated pairs, line abreast as shown in Figure 15.

This had evolved from their experience in the Spanish Civil War and had been devised by the outstanding German fighter ace and tactician, Werner Molders. A photograph of Werner Molders, the ace German fighter pilot, with Field Marshal Herman Goering is shown in Fig.11.

Figure 15 shows the Luftwaffe's basic "Schwarm" formation. The basic formation of four aircraft, or "schwarm", comprised two pairs of aircraft, each pair was known as a "rotte"

The aircraft fly in pairs with the leader of each pair slightly in front and his wingman slightly above him. Each watches the other's side so they have nearly 360 degrees coverage in all directions. The leader of the pair carries out the attack; the task of his wingman is to defend him. The two pairs are in a loose line abreast formation, all at slightly different heights.

A "staffel", or squadron, flew in three fairly widely spaced "schwarms" in a loose line abreast formation, and at slightly different heights to each other.

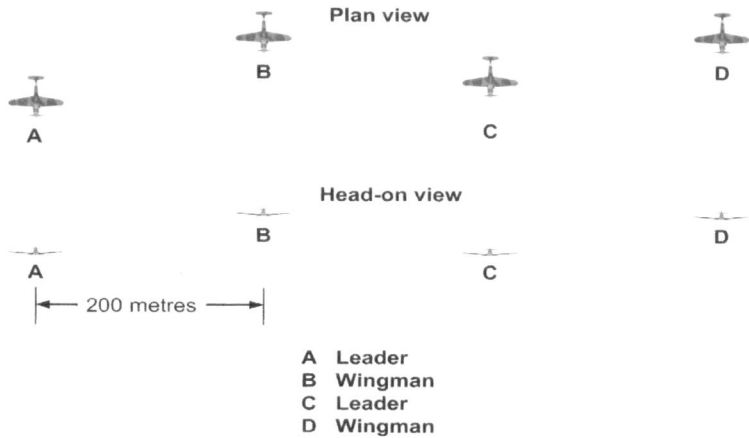

Plan view

B

A

C

D

Head-on view

B

A

C

D

|← 200 metres →|

A Leader
B Wingman
C Leader
D Wingman

Fig. 15 The Luftwaffe's "Schwarm" Formation

(Photograph by courtesy of the Imperial War Museum, London   CH 8119)

Fig. 16   Group Captain A.G "Sailor" Malan

Squadron Leader "Sailor" Malan, the South African fighter ace and Commanding Officer of 74 Squadron,, photograph Fig. 16, adopted the German loose pair formation early on in the Battle.

He called it the "Finger Four" formation. The name arose from describing the formation using four fingers of the hand.

Most RAF squadrons adopted it as the Battle progressed.

He formulated what he called his basic rules of air combat and instilled them into his pilots. He was a fine leader of great skill and determination. Group Captain "Sailor" Malan, as he later became, was one of the RAF's outstanding fighter aces and tacticians in WW 2 and shot down a total of 32 aircraft.

4. 2 Deflection Shooting Skills

A major deficiency on the part of the RAF, which could have been avoided, was the very limited air to air gunnery practice and training the fighter pilots received. All too often, inexperienced pilots would get into a good firing opportunity and miss the target when they opened fire. The aces on both sides were natural shots.

Both sides had simple reflector gun sights to help the pilot aim the aircraft and judge the amount to aim ahead of the enemy aircraft and when to open fire so that it flew into the bullet stream.

This amount depends on the rate of turn of the target sight line and the time of flight of the bullets to reach the target. The bullet time of flight is governed mainly by the target range and the muzzle velocity. Estimating range is thus critical.

Figure 17 (a) illustrates the basic principles of deflection shooting.

Figure 17 (b) is a photograph of a Reflector Gun-Sight.

The reflector gun sight projects the collimated image of an aiming circle directly into the pilot's field of view. The centre of the aiming circle is the aircraft "bore -sight", that is the direction in which the aircraft fore and aft axis is pointing

(The term is based on the analogy of sighting through the bore of a gun barrel mounted on the aircraft datum axis.)

Because the image is collimated, that is focused at infinity, the aiming circle overlays the distant scene and does not move, if the pilot moves his head up or down or side to side, enabling the pilot to aim the aircraft with high accuracy.

The Reflector Gun-sight is, in effect, a fixed symbol Head Up Display, or HUD, and the direct ancestor of the modern HUD.

Figure 17 (c) shows the view through the reflector gun-sight.

Referring to Figures 17 (a), and 17 (c), the pilot manoeuvres his aircraft to track the target through the sight, keeping the aiming circle in front of the target and judges how much to aim ahead and when to fire from the rate at which the target sight line is turning and the range.

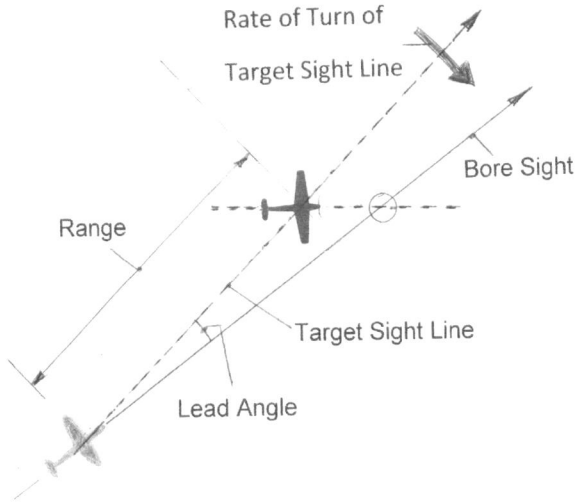

Fig 17 (a)   "Deflection shooting

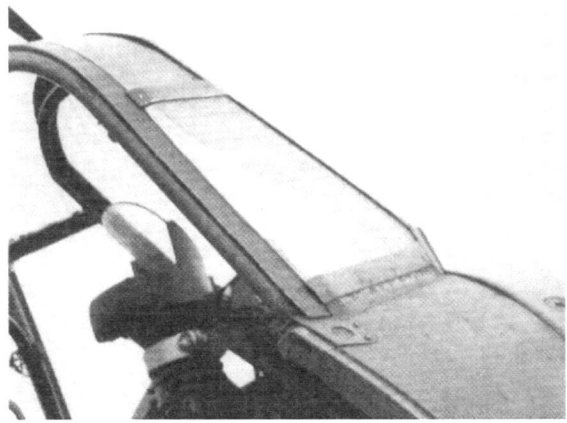

Fig. 17 (b) Reflector Gun Sight

   The small circle on the sight display (Figure 17 (c)) defines the aircraft bore-sight and is referred to as the aiming circle.
The outer circle is a ranging circle to enable the target range to be estimated. (Note: only one ranging circle is shown for clarity.)

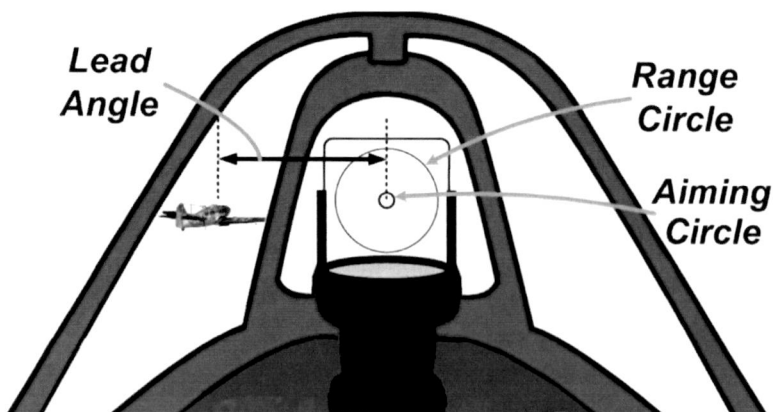

Fig. 17 (c) View through Reflector Gunsight

The ranging circle defines the angle from the bore sight, for example, +/- 20 milli-radians from the bore sight, that is, 40 milli radians across the diameter of the ranging circle, or 2.4 degrees approximately.

The wing tips of an aircraft with a wing span of 10 metres, for example, the Messerschmitt Me 109 E, would just fit inside a range circle of 40 milli-radians diameter at 250 metres range.

(This method of estimating range is known as "stadia-metric ranging", and is still used as a reversionary weapon aiming mode.)

Deflection shooting with the aid of the sight, however, required considerable practice and experience. The RAF fighters had a proportion of 0.303 inch calibre "De Wilde" incendiary bullets in the ammunition belts feeding the wing mounted machine guns. These bullets could ignite fuel tanks if they hit them. The flash when they hit the aircraft also showed the pilot he was aiming correctly. They were of considerable value in improving weapon aiming.

4. 3 The Surprise Attack or "Bounce"

The most common cause of being shot down was the surprise attack – being "bounced", an expression the RAF use to this day. It is absolutely vital for fighter pilots to be constantly scanning for enemy aircraft in all directions, particularly from behind and out of the sun.

Many of the German aces built up their scores by their skills in carrying out a "bounce attack. Young, inexperienced RAF pilots were particularly vulnerable in their early combats. It was a case of learning quickly to survive.

4. 4 The Head-on Attack

A new tactic was introduced by "Treble One" (No. 111) Squadron of the RAF, who flew Hurricanes.
This was the head-on, line abreast, attack on the enemy bomber formations. It took a lot of nerve, or "bottle" to use a current colloquialism, but the results were impressive.
The Treble One pilots reported seeing the bomber pilots trying to get up out of their seats to get out of the bullet stream. The head-on attacks also broke up the bomber formations so that the separated bombers became stragglers and were easily dealt with.
The down side was the inevitable mid-air collisions.
The tactic did not become widespread.

4. 5 Precision, Very Low Level, High Speed Attacks.

On their side, the Luftwaffe introduced precision very low level, high speed attacks using a special elite Group flying Messerschmitt Me 110 fighter-bombers and Dornier Do 17 bombers. They were highly effective; a relatively small force was able to do a lot of damage to the key sector airfields.
The RAF's strategy of high speed, very low level, terrain following strike attacks is basically a modern version of what the Luftwaffe did in 1940.

5. THE AIRCRAFT IN THE BATTLE

The capabilities and performance of the RAF fighter aircraft and the Luftwaffe's fighters and bombers had a direct influence on the Battle.

5. 1 The RAF & Luftwaffe Fighters

During the Battle, the RAF's principal fighter aircraft were the Hawker Hurricane and the Vickers Supermarine Spitfire.
The Boulton Paul Defiant single engine, two seat fighter, which was armed with four 0.303 machine guns in a power operated gun turret, was found to be unsuitable, as mentioned earlier.

The two Defiant squadrons suffered heavy losses in combat with the Messerschmitt Me 109 E early in the Battle and were progressively withdrawn from daytime operations and modified to take on a night fighter role.

The Luftwaffe's principal fighter was the Messerschmitt Me 109 E. The Messerschmitt Me 110 two seat, twin engine escort fighter was used initially with the Me 109 E, but was withdrawn because of the heavy losses experienced in combat with the Hurricanes and Spitfires.

- **Hawker Hurricane**

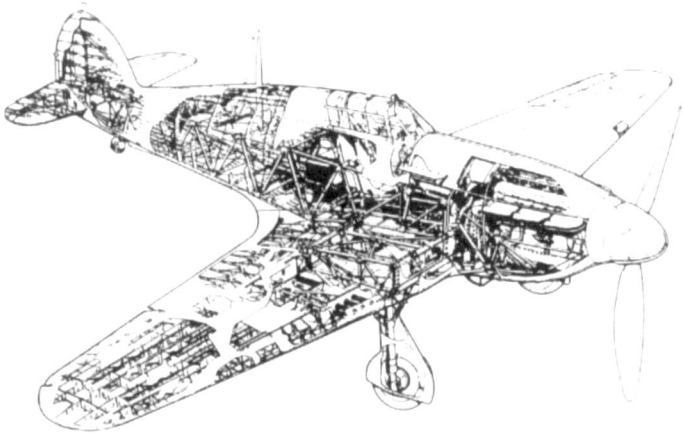

Fig. 18 Hawker Hurricane

The Hawker Hurricane was the backbone of Fighter Command. It equipped two thirds of the fighter force; only one third of the squadrons had the Spitfire. Hurricanes shot down around 70% of the total Luftwaffe aircraft shot down during the Battle of Britain.

The RAF would have lost the Battle without it.

The Hurricane was easy to manufacture and easy to repair. It was also very strong and robust structurally and could withstand battle damage which would have written off a Spitfire, or a Messerschmitt Me109.E. Hurricanes were able to withstand "g" forces pulling out of a dive which would have ripped off the wings of a Me 109 E. The "cut-away" illustration of the Hurricane, Figure 18, shows the simple construction. The rear fuselage was a simple steel tube frame structure and was fabric covered.

It had outstanding manoeuvrability and, in fact, was the most manoeuvrable of the three principal fighters in the Battle. It was easy to fly with vice-less characteristics.

It had a smaller turning circle than the Me 109 E at all altitudes. This is an important advantage in a dogfight, as it enables the pilot to evade an attack as his attacker cannot turn his aircraft at a high enough rate of turn to aim ahead of his target. The aircraft with the higher rate of turn is also able.to get on the inside and behind his opponent as they turn, with a good firing opportunity.

The Hurricane was also a very steady gun platform. This was important, as the German bombers generally required a considerable number of hits from 0.303 bullets to bring them down. The robust wide track undercarriage made it easy to land.

Many RAF aces flew the Hurricane and some preferred it to the Spitfire for all the above reasons.

The Hurricane's minus points were that it was about 40 mph slower than the Messerschmitt Me109 E; 316 mph compared to 357 mph. Its rate of climb and dive were also lower and its performance above 20,000 ft. was considerably lower.

- **Vickers Supermarine Spitfire**

The Vickers Supermarine Spitfire had about equal performance, overall, to the Messerschmitt Me.109E; better in some aspects, worse in others. It was essential to the RAF's success.

It could tackle the Me109 E at higher altitudes on more or less equal terms, while the Hurricanes took on the bombers.

Figure 19 shows the characteristic elliptically shaped wing. The thin wing with its elliptical shape gave major aerodynamic advantages. The wing was not easy to manufacture, however, because of the relatively complex structure required to achieve the necessary strength. The manufacturing hours to build the Spitfire were over three times higher than the Hurricane. Manufacturing problems were the reason why there were more Hurricanes than Spitfires during the Battle.

The Spitfire had excellent manoeuvrability and could turn tighter than the Messerschmitt Me.109 E at all altitudes. It was a pilot's aeroplane in every way; they felt it was part of them when they flew it. It was vice-less in its flying characteristics.

(Photograph by courtesy of the Imperial War Museum, London   CH 1367)

Fig. 19 Vickers Supermarine Spitfire Mk 1 A

The pilot had a better field of view than the Me.109 E; the bulged sides of the cockpit canopy aiding downward vision.

The Spitfire's minus points were that the rate of climb and dive were lower than the Me.109E. Above 20,000 ft. the Me.109E had the edge because its Daimler Benz engine gave more power than the Rolls Royce Merlin engine in the Spitfire, at that time.

The narrow track undercarriage on the Spitfire required care on landing. The view over the nose was poor when landing and pilots executed a side-slip approach to see the runway.

The Spitfire had a further limitation; the ailerons became ineffective when the aircraft reached an indicated airspeed of over 400 mph in a dive, and the aircraft could not be turned.

This was because the fabric covered ailerons ballooned out at high speed and exerted zero rolling moment. The aircraft could not be banked and aircraft need to bank in order to turn. It thus lost vital manoeuvrability when high indicated airspeeds were reached. Very fortunately, the Me.109 E had the same problem.

The problem was later solved in both aircraft by replacing the fabric covered ailerons with metal skinned ones.

Both the Spitfire and Hurricane had a further shortcoming in that the Rolls Royce Merlin engine could cut-out when the aircraft was put into a dive. The negative "g" experienced during this manoeuvre starved the carburettor of petrol causing the engine to cut-out. The total loss of power till the engine re-started could be disconcerting, to say the least. A partial cure was made by fitting a restricting orifice in the fuel line to the carburettor.

The Daimler-Benz engine in the Messerschmitt Me.109 E did not cut-out, as it had a fuel injection system,

Experiencing "negative g", however, is very uncomfortable and can result in nausea. This limits the amount of negative g that can be tolerated to generally considerably less than -1g. Rolling the aircraft through 180 degrees and executing the dive inverted, however, enables the aircraft's flight path to be turned into a steep, near vertical dive at a rate corresponding to a 5 to 6g.turn.((pilot's black-out threshold). This is a much quicker process and was generally adopted when a steep dive to evade an attack was required.

It should be noted that some Hurricanes and Spitfires were fitted with a 20 mm cannon in each wing. The installation proved unreliable and the cannons sometimes failed to fire. The cannons were removed, after the pilot's complained bitterly, and the Browning 0.303 machine guns put back. The installation problems were overcome but not in time for the Battle of Britain.

- **Boulton Paul Defiant**

The Boulton Paul Defiant, shown in Fig. 20, was a two seat fighter armed with four Browning 0.303 machine guns in a power operated turret. It equipped two squadrons of Fighter Command, as mentioned earlier.

It had performed well at Dunkirk and shot down a number of Messerschmitt 109's. The Luftwaffe fighter pilots had mistaken the Defiants for Hurricanes and attacked the Defiants from above and behind. This had disastrous consequences for the Me 109's when the Defiant gunners opened up with their four Browning machine guns in the power operated turret. The Luftwaffe pilots, however, had learned their lesson. On the 19 July 1940, a formation of twelve Me 109's attacked a formation of nine Defiants from behind and underneath them; the Defiant's blind spot. They shot down five Defiants and damaged two others. After this episode, the Defiants were progressively withdrawn for conversion to a night fighter role.

The Defiants did, however, make a few interceptions in August 1940. The Dornier 17, which was recently recovered from the sea bed on the Goodwin Sands in June 2013, was shot down on 26 August 1940 by a Defiant fighter from Hornchurch.

Fig. 20   Boulton Paul Defiant two seat fighter

- **Messerschmitt Me 109 E**

The Messerschmitt Me.109 E was the principal German fighter aircraft during the Battle of Britain. (It should be noted that it used to have the pre-fix "Bf.", Bayerische Flugshafn. This was changed to "Me." during WW 2 and the later prefix is used in this booklet.)
It was one of the best fighters in the world in 1940, when flown by an experienced pilot.

It was the smallest of the three fighters with a wingspan of 9.89 m. (32 ft. 5 in.) compared with 11.23 m. (36 ft. 10 in.) for the Spitfire and 12.19 m. (40 ft 0 in.) for the Hurricane. It was also the lightest of the three fighters. The Me 109 E's performance advantages were rather played down and weaknesses emphasised, at the time, for reasons of morale. It was, however, a brilliant design in concept and execution, and exploited advanced aerodynamic features (for the time), such as a relatively thin wing and leading edge slats. The design achieved a relatively low structure weight which combined with the small frontal area and powerful Daimler Benz 1,100 HP engine gave it an outstanding performance in terms of acceleration, rate of climb and dive and top speed. The manufacturing costs were relatively low; about a quarter of the cost of the Spitfire. Figure 21 shows the compact design. Note: the photograph is of the later Messerschmitt Me 109 G. Photograph on the inside back cover shows the Me 109 E; the external differences from the Me 109 G are fairly small.

(Photograph taken at a WW 2 "Fighter Meet" at Duxford, by the Author)

Fig. 21   Messerschmitt Me 109

The internal detail design was very good: components and equipment were neatly arranged and readily accessible; better in fact than the Hurricane and Spitfire.

The Me 109 E had the heaviest armament of the three fighters; two 20 mm cannon, one in each wing, and two 7.62 mm machine guns mounted on top of the nose and synchronised to fire through the propeller. The Spitfire and Hurricane had eight 0.303 inch calibre Browning machine guns; mounted four in each wing.

A hit from a 20 mm cannon shell, however, did very much more damage than a hit from a 0.303 inch bullet. A three second burst of fire from the Me 109's guns hit the target with 19 lb weight of shells and bullets, compared with 13 lb of bullets in the case of the Hurricane and Spitfire. The cannons, however, had been modified to fit in the Me 109 E's wings and had a shortened barrel and reduced propellant charge together with a modified more compact breech block. These modifications reduced the muzzle velocity and the shells did not do as much damage as the standard 20 mm cannon.

Many of the Hurricane and Spitfires had their guns set so that the bullets from their eight, wing mounted machine guns converged at 200 yards range. The high rate of concentrated fire of the eight machine guns could cause devastating damage when attacks were made at 200 yards range. There wasn't that much difference in the effectiveness of their armaments at close range.

The Daimler Benz engine had a larger capacity than the Rolls-Royce Merlin; 34 litres compared with the Merlin's 25 litres. This combined with fuel injection, made it the more powerful of the two engines, particularly above 20,000 ft. The Me 109 E cockpit was much more cramped than the Hurricane or Spitfire.

The aircraft was generally pleasant to fly, but did have some unpleasant stalling characteristics, if it was allowed to get into a stall. Too tight a turn, when the maximum lift was being reached, could result in one wing stalling before the other, if the leading edge slat on one wing opened before the slat on the other wing. The stalled wing would drop suddenly causing the aircraft to flick over with little or no warning. This limited the turning circle.

Some Me 109 E pilots were also concerned about the aircraft's structural integrity in high g manoeuvres due to structural failures which had occurred in the early development phase of the aircraft.

A stall during the landing approach combined with the very narrow track undercarriage resulted in a lot of landing accidents – most were write-offs.

• The Decisive Factor - The Pilot

It can be seen that the principal fighters, the Hurricane, Spitfire and Messerschmitt 109 E were roughly matched overall.

For example, the outstanding manoeuvrability and structural strength and ability to absorb battle damage of the Hurricane compensating for its lower speed.

The decisive element in most air combats is the pilot. The key factors which govern the outcome of most fighter combats, when the fighters are fairly evenly matched are:
  • The determination and aggressiveness of the pilot.
  • Combat experience.
  • Flying skills.
  • Situational awareness.
  • Deflection shooting ability.
  • Knowledge of the strengths and weaknesses of own and opponent's aircraft.

The old adage about the outcome of a fight between two dogs, "It's not the dog in the fight, but the fight in the dog", can be applied to an aerial "dogfight".

Fig. 22   Messerschmitt Me 110 fighter

• **Messerschmitt Me 110**

The Luftwaffe started the Battle using the Messerschmitt Me 110 twin engine, two seat escort fighters alongside the Messerschmitt 109 E fighter squadrons. The Messerschmitt 110, illustrated in Fig. 22, was fast and heavily armed but it had poor acceleration and a large turning circle compared with the Hurricane and Spitfire. The Me 110's sustained such heavy losses in combat with the RAF that they were withdrawn from the fighter role in the Battle.

It was used very effectively, however, as a fighter-bomber for high speed, low level precision attacks on key sector airfields by an elite strike squadron.

5. 2 The Luftwaffe Bombers

The lesson learned by both sides in WW2 was that bombers operating in daylight were highly vulnerable to determined attacks by faster single seat fighters.

They required escort fighters of comparable performance to the enemy fighters in a ratio of about two fighters to each bomber. Even then, the attrition rate would become unacceptable if the assaults became protracted.

The Luftwaffe used three types of twin engine bomber during the Battle of Britain, namely, the Heinkel He 111, the Junkers Ju 88 and the Dornier Do 17 Z.

They also used the single engine Junkers Ju 87 "Stuka" dive bomber, illustrated in Fig.23, in the initial phases of the Battle.

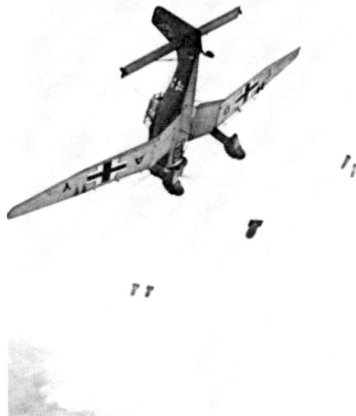

(Photograph by courtesy of the Imperial War Museum, London   GER 18)

Fig. 23   Junkers Ju 87 "Stuka" dive bombe

The Junkers 87 had previously been used with devastating effectiveness in the Battle of France. They were, however, relatively slow, lacked manoeuvrability and were lightly armed.
They were easy targets for the Hurricanes and Spitfires and suffered such heavy losses that they were withdrawn and took no further part in the Battle.
  A common feature of the twin engine bombers was their inadequate defensive armament. This generally comprised 6 to 8 free mounted 7.62 mm calibre drum fed machine guns; the saddle type drums only held 25 rounds of ammunition. They lacked power operated gun turrets with belt fed machine guns.
They were all very vulnerable to determined attacks by the Hurricanes and Spitfires.

- **Heinkel He 111**

Over 500 Heinkel He 111's,(Photograph Fig. 24), were in service with the three Luftwaffe Air Fleets and they comprised over 40% of the Luftwaffe's force of twin engine bombers in the Battle of Britain. The Heinkel 111 carried a bomb load of 4,000 lb; it was not as fast as the Junkers 88, or the Dornier 17, but was well protected by armour plate at vulnerable areas and had self- sealing fuel tanks.

Fig. 24   Heinkel He 111's in formation

It was armed with up to 8 free mounted 7.62 mm calibre drum fed machine guns.

- **Junkers Ju 88**

Fig. 25   Junkers Ju 88

The Junkers Ju 88, (Fig. 25), had an excellent overall performance and was a true multi-role aircraft, able to carry out the roles of bombing, dive-bombing and reconnaissance.

It carried a 4,000 lb bomb load and was the most effective bomber used in the Battle of Britain. The Hurricane had a job to overhaul it in a stern chase. It was armed with 7 free mounted 7.62 mm calibre drum fed machine guns.

- **Dornier Do.17**

(Attribution: Bundesarchiv, Bild 1011-342-0603-25 / Ketelhohn (Krttelhohn) CC-\\\\by-SA)

Fig. 26 Dornier Do.17

The Dornier 17, shown in Figure 26, was fast, capable of nearly 300 mph in a shallow dive, but only carried a 2000 lb. bomb load and had limited defensive fire power. It was nicknamed the "flying pencil" because of its very slim fuselage. It was popular with the Luftwaffe aircrews and had a strong structure. It was armed with 6 free mounted 7.62 mm calibre drum fed machine guns.

There was an elite special Group equipped with the Dornier 17 and the fighter bomber version of the Messerchmitt 110 which carried out the precision low level attacks on the sector airfields.

6. RAF BOMBER COMMAND

The part played by RAF Bomber Command in the Battle of Britain in 1940 should be acknowledged. Their night bombing raids on Berlin at the end of August 1940 were a big factor in the crucial decision to switch the major assaults by the Luftwaffe on the airfields, to an all-out Blitz on London.

They also bombed the invasion barges being assembled in the

Channel ports and the Luftwaffe airfields

RAF Bomber Command sustained substantial losses in these daylight raids and displayed great bravery in carrying out their attacks. They lost over 300 aircraft and 1300 aircrew were killed, wounded or taken prisoner; higher losses in terms of aircrew than RAF Fighter Command.

7. THE GERMAN LUFTWAFFE

The German Luftwaffe failed to win the Battle of Britain and gain air superiority over Britain by destroying the RAF as an effective fighting force in 1940. The losses inflicted by the RAF on the Luftwaffe aircraft in the mass day light raids were unsustainable.

They had to switch to a massive night time Blitz on the major British cities. They regarded the massive night Blitzes, which lasted from September 1940 to June 1941, however, as the continuation of the Battle of Britain

It is appropriate, at this point, to comment briefly on the human side of the Luftwaffe pilots and aircrew who took part in the Battle of Britain. They were led by ardent Nazis, and probably about 10 to 20% were committed Nazis. The majority, however, were not members of the Nazi Party, but were not opposed to them either, at that time. Under Hitler, the German economy and infrastructure had been transformed; their armed forces had defeated the French and British armies and they were now the masters of the whole of Western Europe. Luftwaffe morale was very high in 1940.

It should also be appreciated that any criticism of Hitler, or the Nazi Party, was not exactly a "good career move", to say the least!

The majority of the Luftwaffe pilots and aircrew were patriotic young Germans who were not interested in the Nazi movement. Their overwhelming interest was in flying; they were not very different in many ways from their counterparts in the RAF. The real difference was they were fighting for a monstrous regime.

The RAF pilots were fighting to defend their families and country from Nazi occupation and ultimately to defeat Nazi Germany.

After the war, a number of Luftwaffe ace fighter pilots became better known to the outside world. Many were not Nazis; and were clearly brave, very professional, modest men with likeable personalities. For example, Adolf Galland, Fig. 27, who had the title of "General of Fighters".

Another example was Lieutenant General Gunther Rall, who later became Head of the post-war German Luftwaffe. Both these aces are credited with shooting down over 200 aircraft in WW 2.

Fig. 27 Luftwaffe fighter ace Adolf Galland

8. THE CONTRIBUTORS TO THE BRITISH VICTORY

It is appropriate to comment briefly on all the people and forces in the UK who contributed to the British victory in the Battle of Britain.

- **The Fighter Pilots.**

The courage of the pilots in RAF Fighter Command cannot be praised too highly. They were nearly always outnumbered and fought under tremendous pressure, putting their life on the line three or four times a day, at the height of the Battle.

The number of fighter pilots in Fighter Command who fought in the Battle was just under 3000. Over 500 pilots were killed and many more were seriously injured, badly burned or wounded. Winston Churchill's famous speech on 20 August 1940 summed up the situation superbly, as only he could do, in the phrase: *"Never in the field of human conflict was so much owed by so many to so few"*.

About 80% of the fighter pilots came from the United Kingdom; the rest came from all over the world. Pilots came from what was then the British Empire – from Canada, Australia, New Zealand, South Africa and Rhodesia; some had their own squadrons.

Some of the fighter pilots came from Europe from countries which had been occupied by Nazi Germany. Pilots from Poland and Czechoslovakia had their own squadrons which were led by RAF pilots The Polish Squadron, No 303, flying Hurricanes, had the highest score of German aircraft shot down of all the fighter squadrons taking part in the Battle of Britain. There were also pilots from Belgium and France. There were also a small number of pilots from America who had volunteered to serve in the RAF. They were later to form the "Eagle Squadron".

- **The RAF Ground Crews.**

The RAF ground crews, who kept the aircraft serviceable, armed and refuelled, played an absolutely vital role, as mentioned earlier. They displayed great devotion to duty, working very long hours to keep the aircraft serviceable. At the height of the Battle of Britain, they were coping with up to four sorties a day.

They were in very real danger during the airfield attacks and a number were killed and wounded in these assaults.

- **The WAAF.**

The women in the Women's Auxiliary Air Force, WAAF, in the RAF had a vital role In the Battle as Radar Operators in the Radar Stations and Plotters in the Operations Rooms. They were all volunteers and displayed great dedication and guts.

A number were killed and wounded in the sector airfield raids.

- **Anti-Aircraft Command**

The Army provided the Anti-Aircraft Gun defences of the UK and were closely linked to Fighter Command Head Quarters.

A number of German aircraft were shot down during the Battle by the Army anti-aircraft gun batteries.

- **The Royal Navy.**

The Royal Navy played an absolutely pivotal role in the Battle of Britain as the major deterrent to invasion. The German Army would not attempt a seaborne invasion without first securing air supremacy.

Fifty pilots from the Royal Navy Fleet Air Arm joined the RAF fighter squadrons during the Battle.

- **The Observer Corps**

The vital role of the Observer Corps has been described earlier. They were all unpaid volunteers and showed great dedication.

- **The Aircraft and Munitions Factory Workers**

Aircraft and munitions production in Britain more than doubled during the Battle of Britain. People worked flat out for very long hours, seven days a week. They made a vital contribution.

- **The British People.**

The British people had the will to fight to the end. Without this, the other contributors would have been of no avail.
Witness the collapse of France in June1940.

9. POSTSCRIPT TO THE BATTLE OF BRITAIN

Dowding and Park were treated very unfairly after the Battle. Their leadership had enabled Fighter Command to defeat the Luftwaffe.
Dowding made all the right decisions and was able to ensure his forces remained effective throughout the fiercest assaults. He was able to deploy a fighter force in the final phase strong enough to deny the Luftwaffe air supremacy.

Dowding was replaced by Air Marshal Sir W Sholto-Douglas and given 24 hours to vacate his office. No official acknowledgement was made of his tremendous contribution.
He retired in 1941.

Keith Park was also very unfairly treated. He was told he was being "rested" and sent to command a Flying Training Group.
His job as Commander in Chief of 11 Group was taken over by his arch-critic, Air Vice Marshal Sir Trafford Leigh - Mallory. Keith Park recovered from this setback and took over the air defence of Malta in 1942, at the most critical time. When Park took over, it looked as if the RAF would be overwhelmed and a parachute invasion of Malta from Italy was imminent. Park transformed the situation and the RAF gained air superiority after very fierce air battles over Malta. His career went on from strength to strength after that.